£160 Basic bushcraft kit

Malcolm Bowler AKA JJR SURVIVAL

Disclaimer: The information contained within this Book is strictly for educational purposes. If you wish to apply ideas contained in this Book, you are taking full responsibility for your actions.

All info was correct at the time of writing this book.

It is possible to make a simple and usable bushcraft / wild camping kit from between £160 to £200 the key to finding the equipment is to look for good deals on usable items , i found most of the items on ebay, amazon, various knife websites and charity shops , i will tell you the source of the items and the search terms i used to find them and any other relevant info.

The items that follow are in no particular order , some are very cheap , some are quite a lot more than the rest and there are many other alternatives to these items too, knives seem to be the most expensive when looking for a decent full tang knife , but the mora knives are very cheap but only have small tangs , some people don't mind this and others do, so i have included both types in the book.

Thc items i mention here will make a basic kit and there are many more items you could add as extras, but i have been out wild camping / bushcrafting with these items many times and have got along comfortably.

If you buy the all the cheaper options mentioned in this book you could easily make a simple bushcraft kit for under £160 , but cheapest isn't alway the best , some items like the ferro rods it doesn't seem to make much difference between what ones you buy , but if you are travelling far or abroad you may need specialist equipment so think carefully about what you need and for what purpose , if you are wild camping / doing bushcraft in the uk most of these items will do fine.

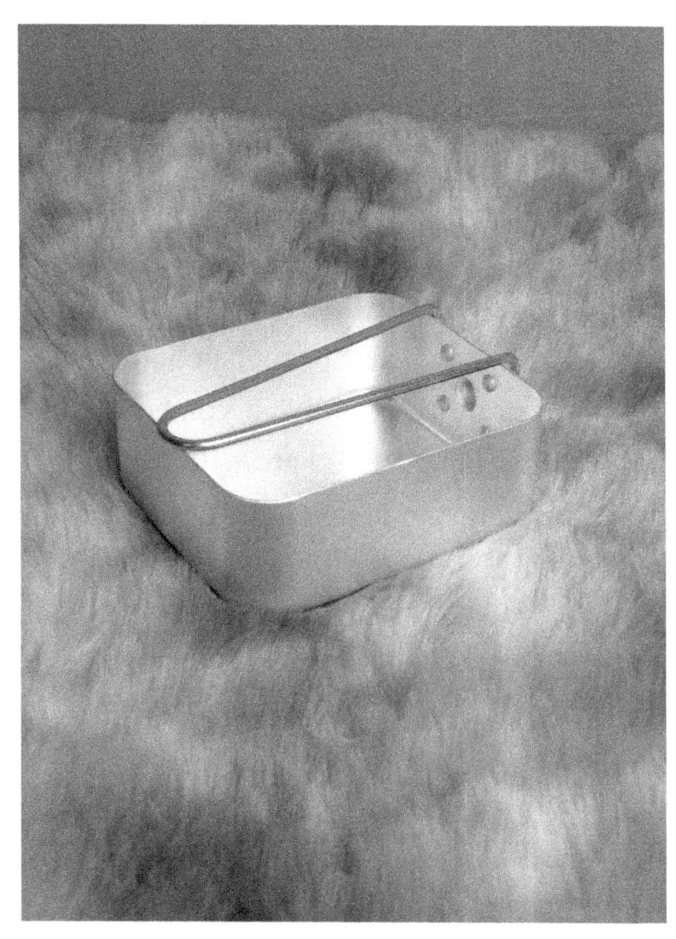

MESS TINS .

SOURCE: ebay , amazon , poundland

SEARCH TERM: mess tins , army mess tins, camping mess tins

PRICE : £1.00 - 2 for £6.00

You may need a mess tin to cook in or boil water , i mention another cook set in the book later, but a cheap mess tins will do if you are on a tight budget , most of the cheap mess tins are aluminium and some people don't like using them , but that is personal preference , if so then look for stainless steel mess tins but no doubt they will be a bit more money (unless you buy from china they are about £15.00 each). You may also want to make a lid when using the mess tins, the simplest way is if you have 2 tins place the larger one over the smaller tin or if you have some tin foil with you make a lid from that .

2.2L bottle
SOURCE: ebay
SEARCH TERM: large water bottle
PRICE : £7.00
You will need a container to carry water so a bottle of some type will be needed , these bottles are quite large and the handle is a good feature ,i will show you metal bottles later in the book , whichever you choose is up to you again , sometimes if i,m going out for a weekend i may just carry water in refilled fizzy drink bottles , but if you want something more permanent choose the biggest bottle you can find for a good price , i don't mention searching for army style bottles because often they are overpriced but these bottles will do and are quite cheap. Depending on where you are going , how long for and if there is a water source you will need to work out how many bottles you will need and if you can carry them as well.

1000ml metal bottles

SOURCE: ebay

SEARCH TERM: metal water bottle , steel water bottle, aluminium water bottle

PRICE :£7.00

Metal water bottles are good especially stainless steel as you may be able to boil water in them directly BUT before you do make sure they don't have a lining inside them , if in doubt just boil in a separate container , also metal is good because it is strong but i found the sizes are always quite limited .

8mm Ferro rod

SOURCE:ebay , amazon

SEARCH TERM: flint striker , ferro rod 8mm ferro rod

PRICE :£3.00

The ferro rod is a great way to start a fire , some preparation will be needed but there is far harder ways to light fires , the good thing about the ferro rod is there is virtually nothing to go wrong or break , unless you lose it , most of the time the cheaper or more expensive ferro rods are no different apart from nicer handles , i have a warning about the handles on the cheaper models, sometimes when striking the rod may fly out of the handle and you will lose it , to stop this happening when you get your cheap ferro rod try to pull out the rod from the handle if it comes out superglue or epoxy it it back in and if it doesn't come out add some superglue anyway just to be on the safe side .

DURONIC
FM AM
108 160
104 129
100 97
96 77
92 63
88 53

Wind up torch / radio
SOURCE: ebay
SEARCH TERM: wind up torch and radio
PRICE :£10 -£15
In the dark at night it pays to have a torch /flashlight of some type ,the radio on this one isn't absolutely needed but could come in handy and being wind-up means you don't need batteries, if you find wind up torches are a nuisance then i'm sure there are many battery powered torches that are as cheap, if not cheaper , also a lamp of some sort can be very handy too .

Paracord

SOURCE: ebay , amazon

SEARCH TERM: paracord , 550 paracord, 100ft paracord

PRICE : £3.00 for 100ft

Paracord is a must if you are setting up a tarp to sleep under , the cheap version of 550 paracord is good enough if you tie the right knots , many people use it and think its good enough too , paracord can also be used for many other things around camp as well. When buying it at the very least make sure it has 7 strands inside , that way the cord can be split apart and you can use the inner strands for other chores as well .

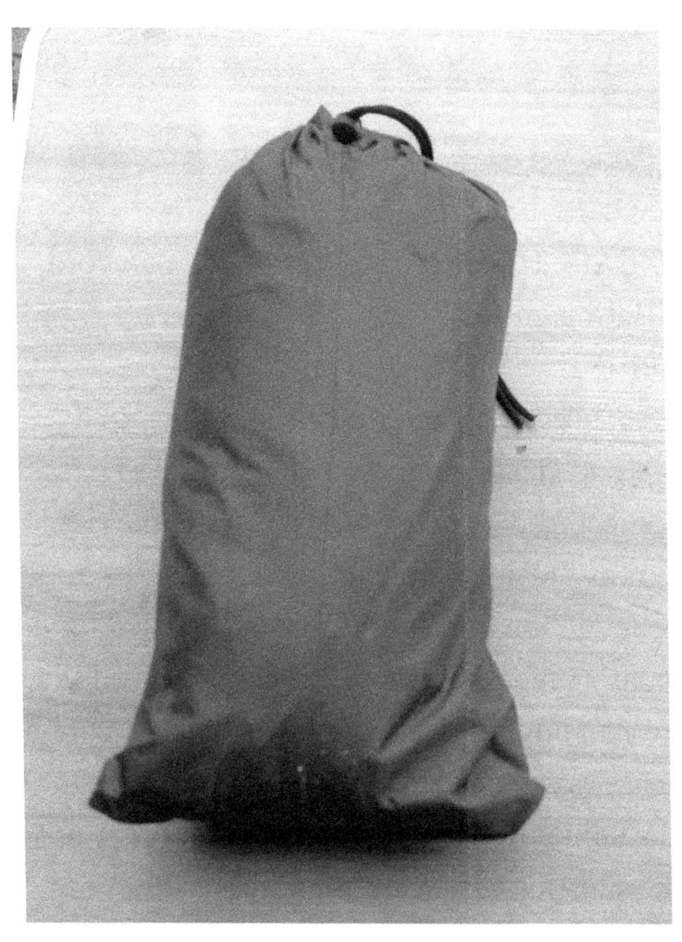

DD camping hammock
SOURCE: ebay , amazon
SEARCH TERM: dd camping hammock .
dd hammocks , camping hammock
PRICE :£25-£30
i chose the dd hammock because it is
something i have used many times and had
no bad experiences with it other a bit of
stitching coming undone after quite a bit of
use , which i just sewed up myself , there are
other cheap hammocks out there but you
will have to check out the reviews of those
as i have no experience with them . By using
a hammock , you eliminate the need for
ground sheets , and sleeping pads/ mats , it
also gets you off the ground and is a much
smaller package to carry with you.
If you don't want to sleep in a hammock you
can replace it with a sleeping mat and a
ground sheet , the sleeping mat you can get
for around £10 and you can buy a smaller
tarp for the ground sheet .

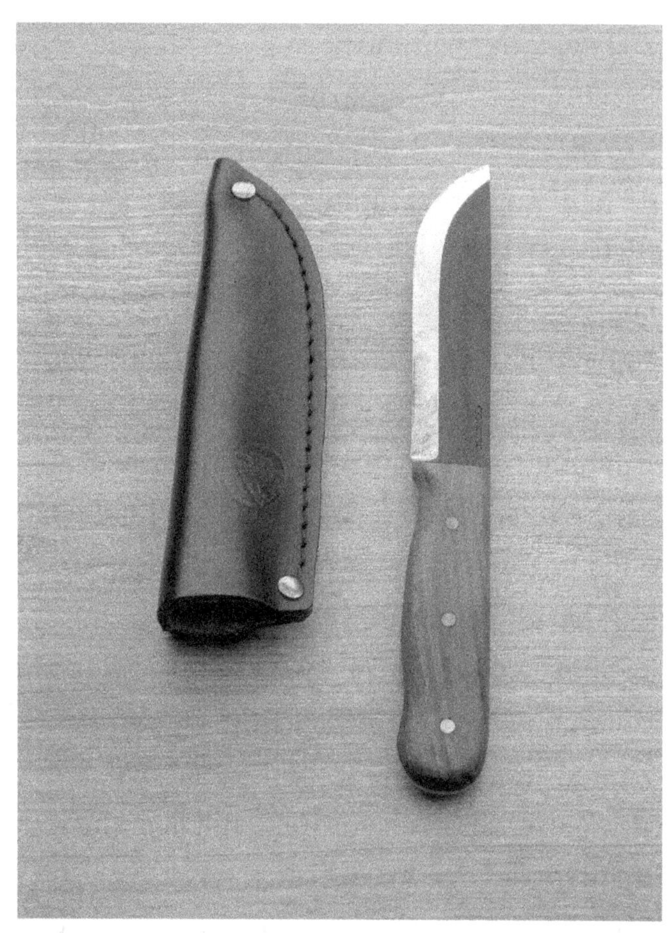

Condor bushcraft knife 5"
SOURCE: heinnie haynes , springfields,
amazon
SEARCH TERM: Condor bushcraft knife 5"
PRICE :£50
Probably the most expensive item in the kit
is the condor bushcraft 5" knife , it is a good
knife , full tang , carbon steel , scandi grind
blade , condor does a better knife the
bushlore but it's a bit more expensive , and
as we are trying to keep cost at a minimum
we'll look at the 5" bushcraft knife . some
people may prefer a blade which is more
pointed , if so then you,ll have to look for
something else , but the 5" bushcraft knife is
a decent knife for the price, it also comes in
other sizes hence the 5" part in the name ,
the handle can be quite smooth and straight ,
so i reshaped mine with a dremel tool but
it's not necessary if you don't want to.

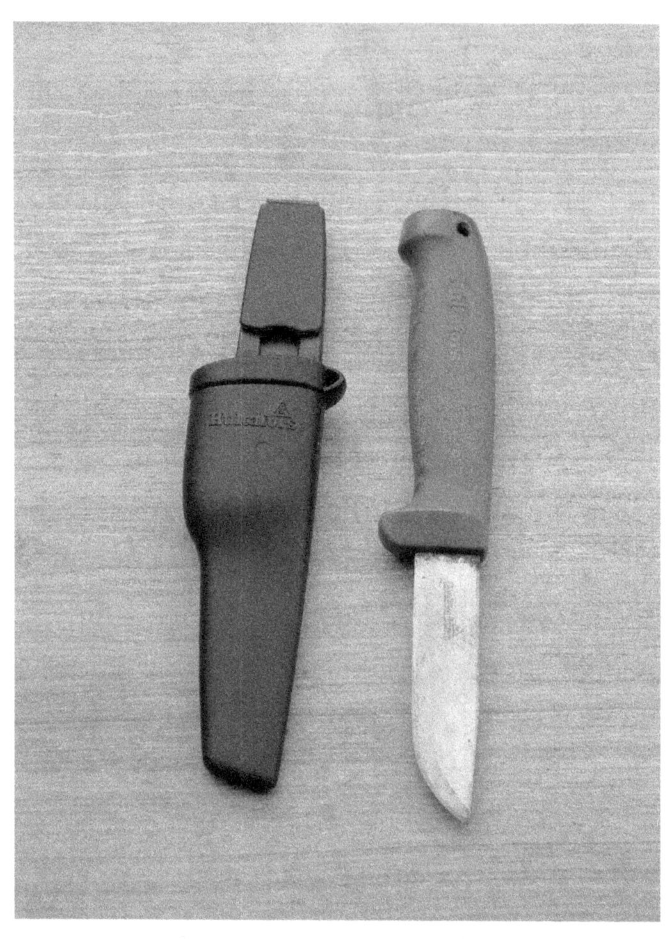

Hultafors hd knife

SOURCE:heinnie haynes , springfields , amazon

SEARCH TERM: hultafors knife , hultafors hd ,hultafors hd knife

PRICE :£8

The hultafors hd knife is a great alternative to the popular mora knives , you can get them for very cheap , they do not have scandi grind blade which a lot of people think they might but they are carbon steel , the tang on the hultafors goes just over halfway in the handle . but they are very strong knives especially for the price . both the hultafors and the moras will need to be filed along the back of the blade to work with your ferro rod as they have round / unfinished spines .

More budget knives : anglo arms desert master , mora 510 , mora hunter
SOURCE: heinnie haynes , springfields
SEARCH TERM: anglo arms desert master, mora clipper , mora knives .
PRICES :£8 - £12
Most of the mora knives are very cheap and are very popular with outdoors enthusiasts , the mora clipper is a popular knife for bushcraft they have scandi grind blades and are carbon and stainless steel ,but most of the moras have only a small tang , but a lot of people swear by them regardless, the anglo arms desert master is full tang, stainless steel and has a micro bevel blade and is quite a cheap knife but it is small as well, i wouldn't hesitate to take it out but maybe not so much as my main knife , i would probably want something a little bigger , as for alternatives i could fill an entire book about knives, but use your own judgement and other peoples recommendations if you want to choose something else .

2.7m x 3m camo tarp

SOURCE: ebay , amazon

SEARCH TERM: camo tarp , 3x3 camo tarp, tarpaulin.

PRICE :£10.00

A tarp/ basha will be needed if you are sleeping in a hammock , you can get purpose made tarps for use with a hammock that have a lot of eyelets / tabs for tying , but they are a lot more expensive than the ones i mention, which is essentially a camo tarpaulin sheet if you rig up the tarp with paracord on each corner and one long line going along the middle these tarps will do just fine, i have slept out in torrential rain under one and it worked fine , when buying always buy slightly bigger than you need as sometimes the size quoted is the size before the ends and sides have been folded and the eyelets added , so it may be smaller than you think it is.

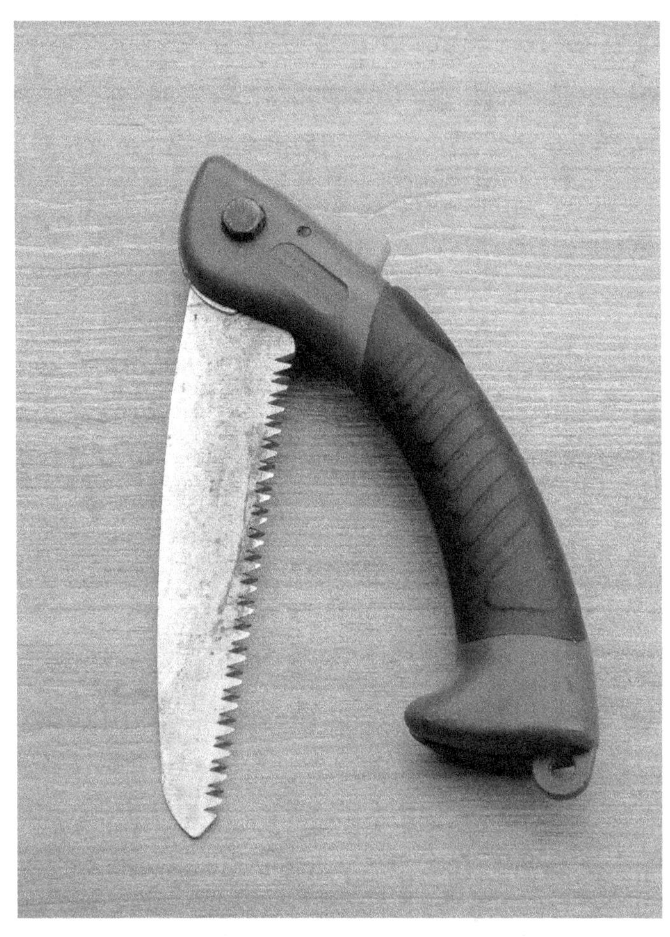

Folding saw

SOURCE:ebay , amazon

SEARCH TERM: pruning saw, folding saw

PRICE :£6.00 - £10.00

A folding saw is a handy item if you are cutting wood, it packs away small and is quite light weight , make sure it has a locking blade and get some practice in using it . you will find an assortment of different colour saws but most will be the same if they are the gardeners / pruning type of saw. As a very cheap alternative you could purchase a bow saw blade and some nuts and bolts and make a handle while out in the woods

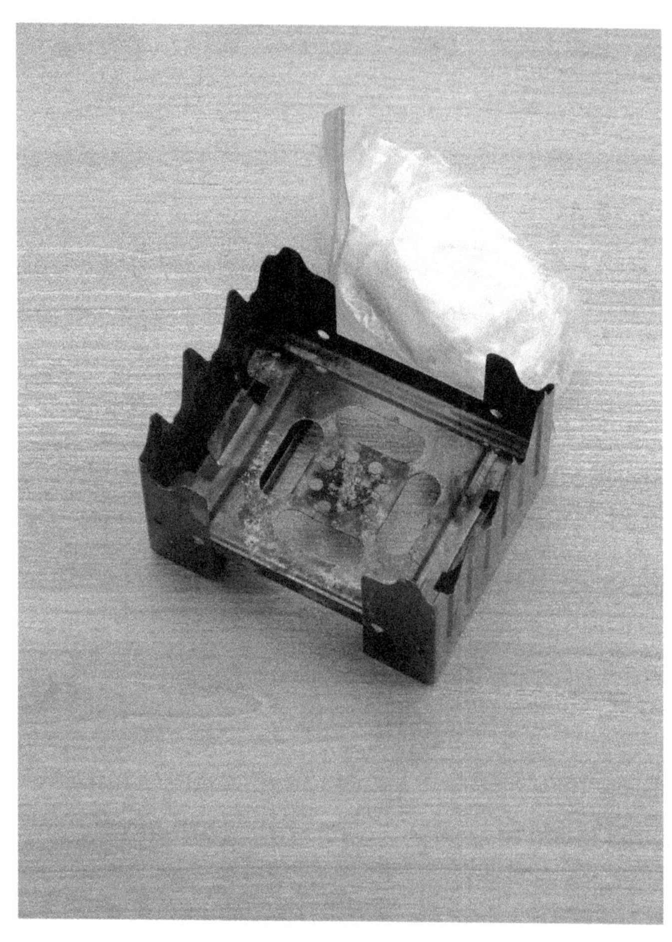

Hexamine stove

SOURCE:ebay , amazon

SEARCH TERM: hexamine stove ,army stove

PRICE :£4.00 - £5.00

Hexamine stoves and fuel tablets are cheap and a small package to carry around. Not the best but they do work pretty good,but you have no control over the heat other than trying to raise your pan higher which you can't do with just the pot holder . but they are simple , you just light a fuel tab and put your pot on the holder . don't use these in a tent or anything, make sure you have good ventilation . you can find quite a lot of alternative stoves and pot holders online, some use just wood like the wood gas stoves others can be used with different fuels , have a look at some reviews and prices if you don't want to use a hexamine stove .

Trangia stove

SOURCE:ebay , amazon

SEARCH TERM: meths stove , alcohol stove trangia stove

PRICE :£8.00

In a bid to keep the price of the kit low i recommend a trangia stove to be used with the hexamine stand , that way you only need to buy the stove itself rather than a whole set, with the trangia stove you will need to carry meths in a small bottle, if you didn't want to use it like this you can just get a set which has a pot holder with it, but the way i mentioned means you have 2 stoves / fuels that can be used with 1 pot holder .

Travel pillow

SOURCE:ebay , amazon

SEARCH TERM: collapsible camping pillow

PRICE :£6.00

a small pillow isn't absolutely necessary if you're sleeping in a hammock , some people like to have one, other don't , i often feel like i don't need it and it can end up anywhere in the hammock overnight. so again this one is personal preference , as well as these types of pillow you can also get blow up / inflatable ones too for quite cheap prices .

Metal cup / canteen cup

SOURCE: ebay , amazon

SEARCH TERM: canteen cup, steel canteen cup, metal cup , metal canteen cup

PRICE :£4.00 - £6.00

A nice metal cup made of stainless steel or aluminium , is a good thing to have , obviously you can drink out of it but you can boil your water for the drink in the cup itself , choose one that has good folding handles and watch your lips when drinking from it if you have just boiled water in it .

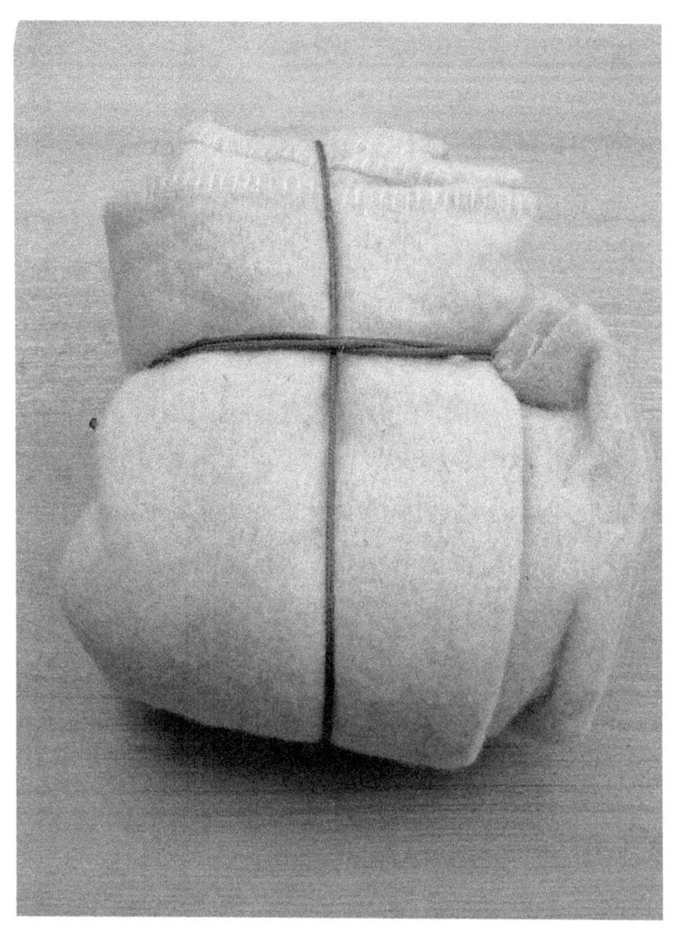

Wool blanket

SOURCE: charity shop

SEARCH TERM: wool blanket

PRICE :£2.00 - £5.00

a wool blanket might be needed depending on what sleeping bag you have , and how cold it is at night , if you have a cheap 4 season sleeping i would take a wool blanket too as a back to the sleeping bag, if not needed in the night you can put it under you inside the hammock as an under blanket , if you have a decent 4 season sleeping you may not need the wool blanket at all . but i take mine just incase , wool is great as even if its wet it will still keep you warm .

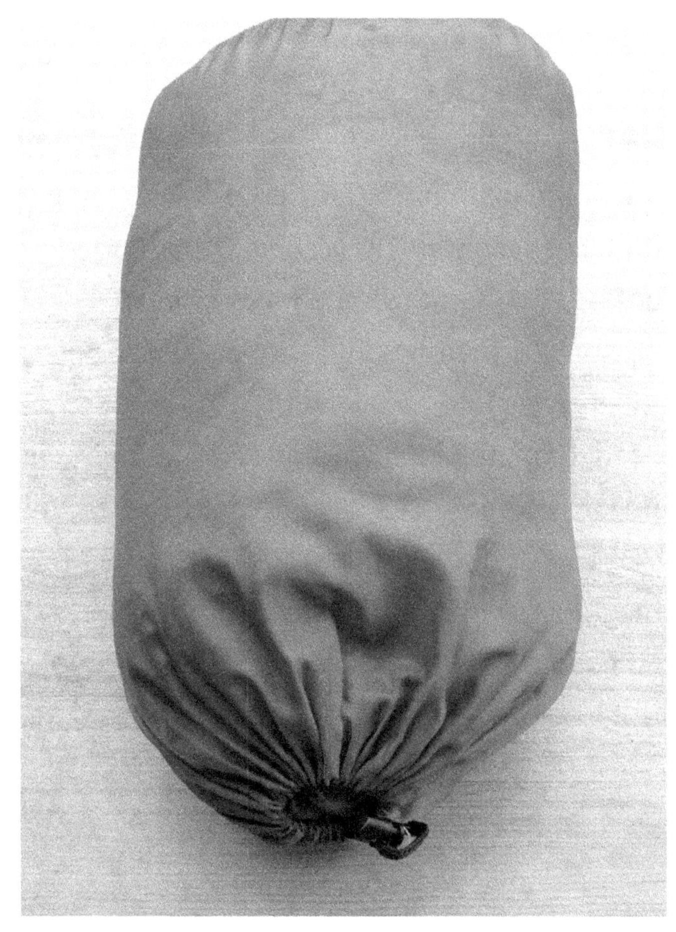

4 season sleeping bag

SOURCE: ebay , amazon

SEARCH TERM: 4 season sleeping bag

PRICE :£10.00 - £30.00

Your sleeping bag is a very important bit of kit so buy the best you can in your budget, it really is another must have if you are sleeping outside, regardless of what time of the year and where you are going get a 4 season sleeping bag or an arctic sleeping bag, army surplus is a great way to get a good arctic sleeping bag. if it's warmer you can open the sleeping bag . mummy or envelope type depends on what you prefer, i prefer the envelope type with a hood when sleeping outside . you can also add your wool blanket if its really cold.

Axe / hatchet

SOURCE:ebay , amazon

SEARCH TERM: small hatchet , small axe hand axe

PRICE :£10.00 - £30.00

You may or may not want to buy an axe or hatchet , it depends on where you are going and if you will be processing firewood , i have been out many times and not used my small hatchet . but if you are going to process wood you will need an axe , if space is a major issue you could get a hatchet like the one pictured , if not you can get a bigger axe , i found most bought online as garden type axes are quite blunt and will need to be sharpened , and a duct tape mask will have to be made for the axe head. An axe with a wooden handle can be replaced if they break and you are good enough at making a new one.

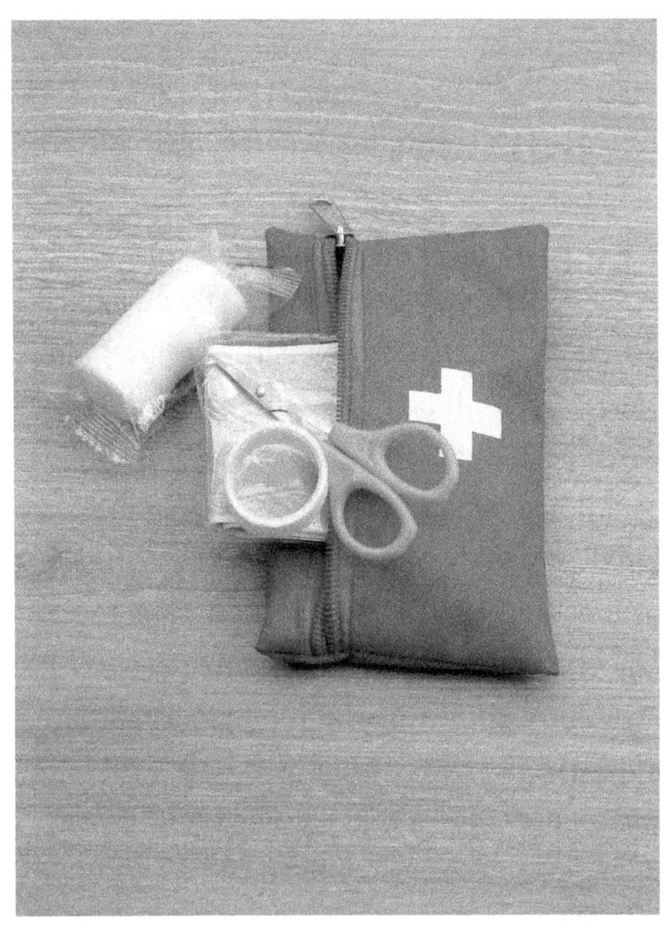

First aid kit

SOURCE:ebay , amazon

SEARCH TERM: first aid kit

PRICE : £2.00 - £20.00

A first aid kit is another must have item if you are going out into the woods with blades or axes, if you know you are not going to do cutting of any sort a small first aid might do, a cheap way to get a first aid kit is to buy a couple of cheap first aid kits and combine them into one then buy any extras that you need to put in . have a look online for what is recommended for a wilderness first aid kit.

as a side note: always take a mobile phone or some sort of communication with you and always tell people where you are going and when you should be back .

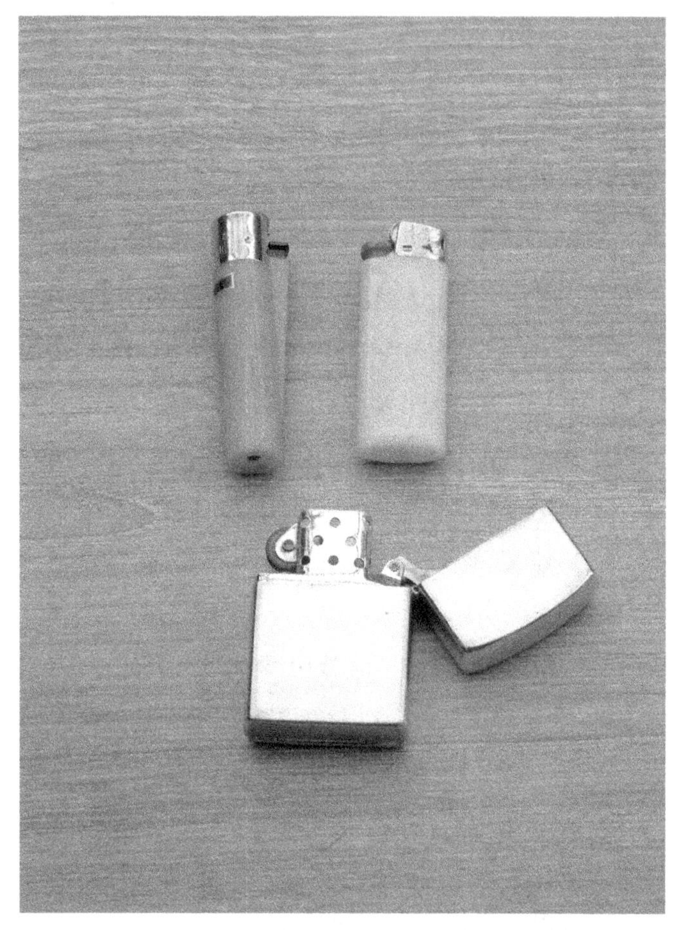

Lighters

SOURCE:ebay , amazon

SEARCH TERM: flip top lighter, clipper lighter . bic lighter .

PRICES : bic £1.00, clipper £1.00, flip top lighter £2.00 -£6.00

By having a couple of different lighters it means you have the ability to light a fire or a stove in an instant rather than having to prepare items to light like you would with the ferro rod . a cheap flip top lighter will work with quite a few different fuels if you pour them directly on the wick (that way it won't ruin the insides) and the flint can be used to ignite tinders , bic lighters are good and cheap but you cannot easily change the flint or refill them , but a clipper lighter is fully refillable and the flint striker can be removed and used to light tinders too.

Cooking set

SOURCE: ebay , amazon

SEARCH TERM: camping cook set, camp cook set ,

PRICE :£7.00 - £20.00

You can buy a set of cooking utensils rather than just a single mess tin , this set has a fork , frying pan / pan lid , pot and a cup , its slightly better quality than the cheap mess tins and has rubber coated handles which fold .you can find these or similar items on ebay and amazon , or local hiking / camping shops .

Rucksacks / backpack
SOURCE:ebay , amazon
SEARCH TERM: 50l rucksack , 60l
rucksack rucksacks
PRICE :£20.00 - £40.00
You will definitely need a rucksack to put
all your items in , personally i found a 50l
bag is big enough to fit all the items i
mention in, a smaller rucksack would work
but the sleeping bag would have to be tied
on top or somewhere on the bag , army
surplus rucksacks are pretty decent and large
but seem to be quite a price compared to
some others , a good camping rucksack will
do the trick , there are many different
rucksacks, some have frames , many
pockets, waist straps etc , but get one that
will fit all your items and is comfortable
and also think about how far you are
travelling with the bag . if you think the bag
is not waterproof buy a liner or use a bin bag
/rubble sack as a liner tied at the top.

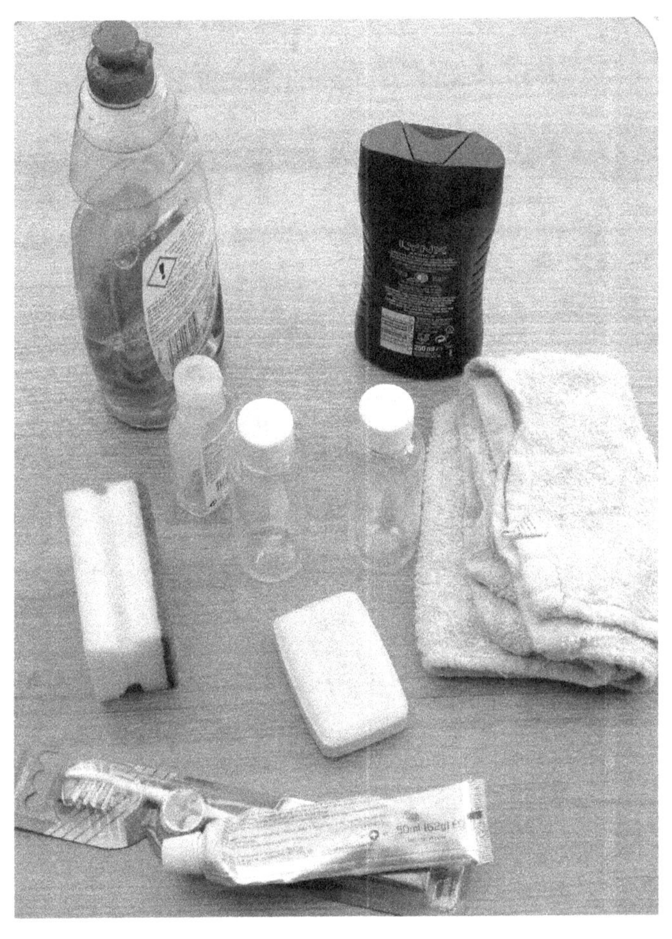

625ml℮
LYNX
AFRICA

Toiletries and cleaning items

SOURCE: ebay

SEARCH TERM: small empty bottle set, sponges , clothes , flannels

PRICE :£2.00 - £5.00

If you want to save some money i thinks its best to just buy or use cleaning / hygiene items in your house and decant the contents into smaller bottles , you can buy a variety of small clear bottles from ebay or amazon , as for the toothbrush cut a bit off the handle and put it in a bag or an empty vitamin tube , also sponges , bars of soap can be cut in half to make them smaller . Alcohol hand gel is a very useful item to carry for minor hand cleaning and can be used as a fire lighter or pour onto the wick of a flip top lighter. Flannels and baby wipes will be handy to have in your kit too also a little trowel for burying any waste is important otherwise make a digging stick to dig the hole .

PEAK
ERY SET
K

Eating utensils

SOURCE:ebay , amazon ,pound shop.

SEARCH TERM: knife fork and spoon set

PRICE :£1.00 - £6.00

You can get a relatively decent little knife ,
fork and spoon set from one of the pound
shops or on ebay , if you really want to be
cheap you can just take a set from home out
of the draw . (just don't let the other half
catch you) and put an elastic band around
them to hold them together then put them in
a bag.

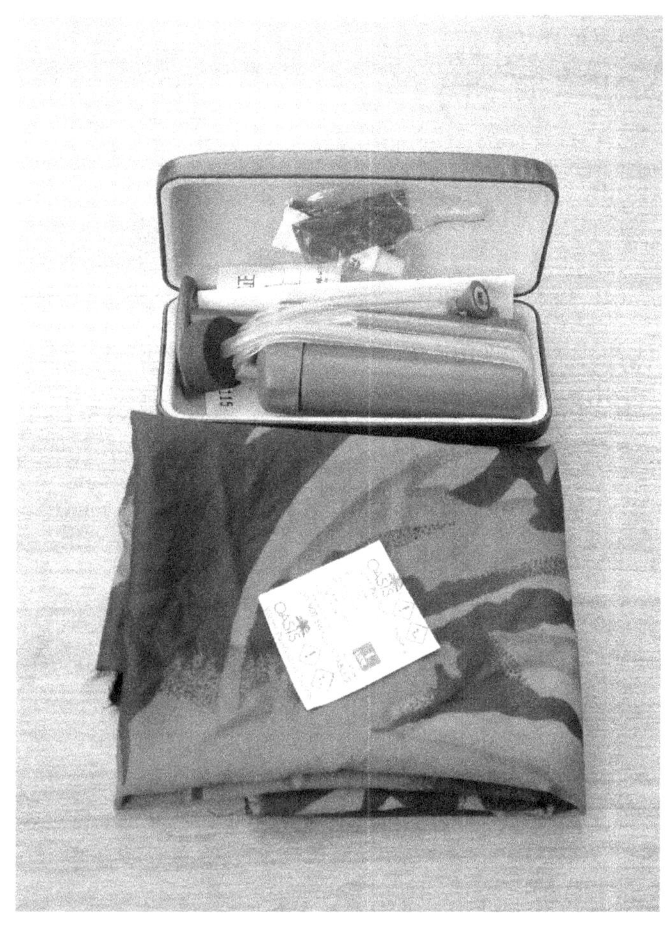

Water purification

SOURCE: ebay

SEARCH TERM: water purifier camping , bushcraft water purifier .water purifications tablets , bandana

PRICE:£2 - £20

If you don't have access to clean water while out you will need a water purifier of some sorts , a pump type is handy, but quite pricey if on a really tight budget , you could also use bandana to strain the water then boil it which many people do , also water purification tabs are very useful and easy to carry . an alternative could be a millbank bag . whatever you buy ,check all instructions and use as recommended .

Extras

The items i mentioned in the previous pages will make a basic bushcraft kit, there are many other items that can be added, it depends on what you are doing and where you are going , if you are travelling far you may need navigation equipment and maps and if you are staying out a long time you may need extra equipment or different equipment, also some other things to consider are ,will you be having a campfire ? if so ,you might not need to buy or take a stove with you , will there be water there ? if not you may want to buy bigger water bottles or extra bottles , have a good think about where you are going and what you may need to take .

some extra items might be :

KNIFE / AXE SHARPENER

LAMP

POCKET KNIFE

HEAD TORCH

WATERPROOF BAGS

WATERPROOF JACKET .

Many thanks for reading my book ,
for more info check out my youtube channel
JJR SURVIVAL

And the other books i have written
REPURPOSED BUSHCRAFT
EQUIPMENT (REVISED).

BASIC SURVIVAL TRAPS.

HOW TO MAKE A NATURAL
SLINGSHOT.

BUSHCRAFT AND SURVIVAL
HUNTING TOOLS.

SURVIVAL TRAPPING, PHEASANT
AND GROUND BIRD TRAPS.

20/8/18